Genre Expository Text

Essential Question

How can a scientific investigation be an adventure?

ADVENTURE UNDER THE ICE

BY MAX OLSEN

Introduction 2

Chapter 1
The Bottom of the Sea 4

Chapter 2
A New Solution 8

Chapter 3
Building a Robot 12

Conclusion 16

Respond to Reading 18

PAIRED READ **What's Bean Happening?** 19

Glossary 22

Index 23

STEM **Focus on Science** 24

INTRODUCTION

Dr. Stacy Kim is a scientist who studies plants and animals that live in the **seabed**. She does her scientific **investigations** in the Antarctic, the most southern place in the world. In such an exciting place, her work is often an adventure.

Dr. Kim has worked in freezing temperatures. She has lived without sunlight for months. She has also discovered new species and seen amazing wildlife.

Dr. Kim wears several layers of clothing to stay warm in the Antarctic.

The Antarctic is a **challenging** place to work. It is difficult because seabed creatures and plants are hidden under thick ice.

Dr. Kim had difficulties reaching the seabed, so she gathered a team of scientists to help her. The team members **collaborated**. They figured out how to overcome this problem. They built a robot for the Antarctic!

Dr. Kim (second from right) and her research team have gone on many scientific missions together.

CHAPTER 1
THE BOTTOM OF THE SEA

Dr. Kim and other scientists study the Antarctic seabed because they want to learn about what lives there. They sometimes discover new plants and animals. In 2010, they discovered a new **carnivorous** sea sponge.

Dr. Kim is interested in seabed ecology. Seabed ecologists are scientists who study what seabed animals eat and how some need others to survive.

Many kinds of plants and animals live on the Antarctic seabed.

Dr. Kim works at McMurdo Station. The station is the **base**, or center, of the United States' Antarctic program. The base used to pollute the sea in this area. It dumped its trash and **sewage** into the water. A new sewage treatment center was built. Studying the seabed can show how the life there is recovering from this pollution.

Scientists are also interested in climate change, or rising temperatures, in the Antarctic. Higher temperatures are causing the ice to melt. Scientists study how climate change affects life in the seabed.

STOP AND CHECK

What are scientists studying at McMurdo Station?

Giant icebergs break off from the ice shelf in the Antarctic.

The Antarctic is the coldest, windiest, and driest place on Earth. The weather is a big challenge for scientists who work there.

McMurdo Station can be as cold as minus 58 degrees Fahrenheit. Scientists have to wear special boots to keep their feet warm and dry. Without these boots, the scientists' socks could get **saturated** with moisture. They also wear suits that protect them from the wind and cold.

It takes a lot of energy to keep warm. Scientists must eat food with plenty of **protein**, such as meat, eggs, and milk.

Sometimes Dr. Kim and her team go on research **expeditions**. They stay in strong, windproof tents.

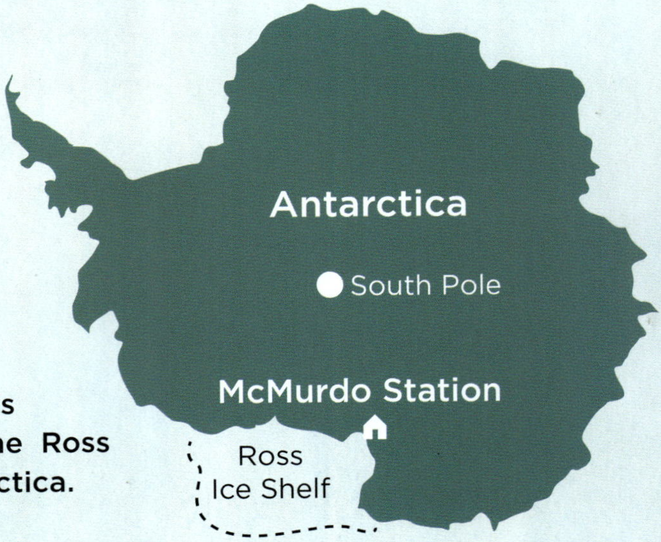

McMurdo Station is on the edge of the Ross Ice Shelf in Antarctica.

Antarctic seasons are another challenge. The sun does not rise in the winter or set in the summer. Scientists have to work in the dark in winter. They have to learn to sleep when it is light outside in summer.

Working in the Antarctic also has rewards. Scientists get to see fascinating wildlife, such as seals and penguins.

STOP AND CHECK

What are some challenges of working in the Antarctic?

The Race to the South Pole

Roald Amundsen, from Norway, led the first expedition to the South Pole in 1911. Amundsen's team traveled on sleds pulled by teams of dogs.

A British expedition, led by Robert Scott, arrived at the South Pole five weeks later. They had wanted to get there first, but they were too late.

Amundsen's sled dogs rest in the Antarctic in 1911.

CHAPTER 2
A NEW SOLUTION

Taking photographs of the seabed can be challenging. In the past, researchers had to cut a hole in the ice and dive into the freezing water.

Today small holes can be made with a drill in less than an hour. However, making a hole big enough for a diver takes much more time and effort.

Researchers use special equipment to drill large holes in the ice.

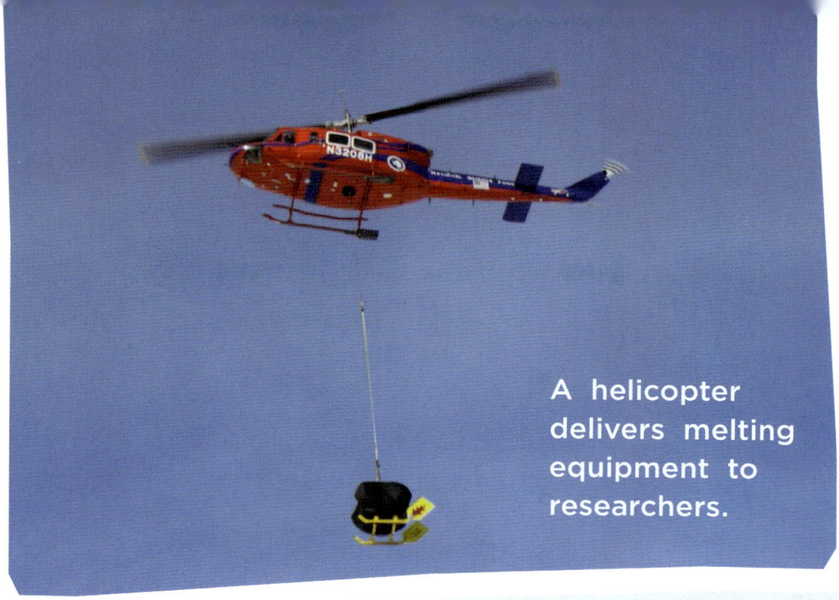

A helicopter delivers melting equipment to researchers.

There are three ways to make a hole in the ice big enough for a diver: drilling, blasting, or melting.

To drill a hole, researchers need a tractor, a large drill, and an electricity **generator**. Each of these machines needs a **specialist**, or expert, to operate it.

To blast a hole, a helicopter brings **explosives**, such as dynamite, to the site. This method cracks the ice around the hole. Broken ice can be dangerous for the researchers. They must wait for it to freeze before using the hole.

Melting the ice needs a generator. The equipment needs to be refueled every three hours.

Making holes to get to the water is a challenge. So is diving in the freezing water. Divers can stay underwater for only a short time. It is unsafe for them to dive deeper than 130 feet. If they go deeper, they may develop **decompression sickness**, or "the bends."

Weddell Seals

Sometimes Weddell seals take over an ice hole that the researchers have made. The divers can't use the hole anymore. Weddell seals need holes in the ice to breathe. They usually make the holes themselves.

Weddell seals occupy holes in the ice.

Dr. Kim thought there must be an easier way to take photographs of the seabed. She came up with an **alternative** plan that didn't need large holes or divers. Her idea was to use a robot that could fit through a smaller hole.

Dr. Kim and her team built this robot. They called it SCINI (pronounced "skinny"). SCINI means **Submersible C**apable of under **I**ce **N**avigation and **I**maging.

STOP AND CHECK

Why is it difficult to take photographs of the Antarctic seabed?

The SCINI robot cruises over the seabed in McMurdo Sound.

CHAPTER 3
BUILDING A ROBOT

The SCINI team included an **oceanographer**, a **software** designer, and a robotics expert.

The team began building the robot in the middle of 2007. They worked quickly because they wanted to use the robot in the next Antarctic summer.

The team first built a **trial** robot to make sure it would work. It was shaped like a long tube so that it could fit through a small hole in the ice.

Summer in Antarctica begins in November.

The team tested the trial robot in a seawater tank. At first, the motors kept breaking down and the photographs were very **blurry**. The researchers needed the motors to be stronger and the photographs to be clearer.

To fix these problems, the researchers put in more **resilient** motors and a better camera. By October, the robot was ready to be used in Antarctica.

Researchers tested SCINI in a seawater tank.

The robot was a great success. It was small and light, so the researchers could transport it by snowmobile.

The team drilled a 6-inch hole in the ice and lowered SCINI into the water. They directed the robot to places that **corresponded** to, or matched up with, places they wanted to photograph on the seabed.

Drilling a small hole for SCINI is much easier than making a large hole for a diver.

SCINI let Dr. Kim study a much larger area of the seabed. Cutting small holes for SCINI took less time. The robot could also go deeper than divers.

SCINI also found experiments that had been "lost" on the seabed. These experiments were started before researchers knew it was dangerous to dive so deep.

Researchers use SCINI near McMurdo Station.

STOP AND CHECK

What can SCINI do?

CONCLUSION

Research has become much easier for seabed scientists. Using SCINI, they can gather information from deeper under the sea. Scientists have learned a lot about life on the seabed from SCINI's photographs.

Scientists no longer need to dive into freezing water to study the seabed. Instead, they can photograph the seabed from the safety of a tent.

Photographs from SCINI show life on the Antarctic seabed.

However, SCINI cannot do everything that a person can do. It cannot **extract** samples. Divers still have to go under the ice to remove samples of rocks, mud, and **foliage**, or plants. They still have to travel over snow and camp out on the ice. Even with the help of a robot, working in Antarctica is a real adventure!

Dr. Kim gets ready to dive with SCINI.

Respond to Reading

Summarize

Use details from *Adventure Under the Ice* to summarize the selection. Your graphic organizer may help you.

Main Idea
Detail
Detail
Detail

Text Evidence

1. Reread pages 4 and 5. What is the main idea? What are two key details that support this idea?
   MAIN IDEA AND KEY DETAILS

2. Find the word *ecologist* on page 4. What clues help you to figure out the word's meaning?
   VOCABULARY

3. Write about how SCINI was improved. Include key details from the text on page 13.
   WRITE ABOUT READING

Genre **Expository Text**

Compare Texts

Read about an experiment where you follow steps to test an idea.

What's Bean Happening?

This experiment shows how fertilizer affects the growth of bean plants.

The Investigation

Four groups of beans are planted. Each group is given a different amount of fertilizer. Fertilizer helps plants grow.

The **hypothesis** of an experiment is what the scientist thinks will be the result. The hypothesis for this study is that the plants that have the most fertilizer will grow fastest.

Materials and Equipment

- 12 plant pots
- a bag of potting mix
- a bag of fertilizer
- 12 bean seeds
- a teaspoon
- a cup
- a windowsill or another sunny place

The Procedure

Step 1

The pots are divided into four groups: Groups A, B, C, and D. There are three pots in each group. Each pot is filled with potting mix.

Step 2

No fertilizer is added to Group A. One spoonful of fertilizer is added to Group B. Three spoonfuls of fertilizer are added to Group C. Six spoonfuls of fertilizer are added to Group D.

Step 3

One bean seed is planted in each pot. The pots are watered every day and left on a windowsill in the sun.

Step 4

The plants are measured after two weeks. Their heights are recorded.

Step 5

The plants are measured after another two weeks. Their heights are recorded again.

Step 6

The average height of each group of pots is calculated. The average heights between the groups is compared.

The Results

The plants in Group C grew the fastest. This means that the hypothesis for the investigation was wrong. The beans with the most fertilizer (Group D) did not grow the fastest. They did not grow at all because there was too much fertilizer. The plants with three spoonfuls of fertilizer grew the fastest.

It was fun waiting to see if the hypothesis would be proven correct or incorrect. This experiment was certainly an adventure!

Experiment Results

Average Height	Group A	Group B	Group C	Group D
after two weeks	1/2 inch	3/4 inch	1 1/4 inches	No Growth
after four weeks	1 inch	2 1/2 inches	4 3/4 inches	No Growth

The plants in Group C grew fastest.

Make Connections

Why did the narrator feel that this experiment was like an adventure? **ESSENTIAL QUESTION**

Describe the different processes used in *Adventure Under the Ice* and *What's Bean Happening*? **TEXT TO TEXT**

Glossary

carnivorous *(kahr-NI-vuh-ruhs)* eating meat ***(page 4)***

collaborated *(kuh-LA-buh-ray-tuhd)* worked together ***(page 3)***

decompression sickness *(dee-kuhm-PRE-shuhn SIK-nuhs)* a condition that occurs when divers return to the surface too quickly ***(page 10)***

expeditions *(ek-spuh-DI-shuhnz)* journeys made for a reason ***(page 6)***

generator *(je-nuh-RAY-tuhr)* a machine that makes electricity, steam, or other energy ***(page 9)***

investigations *(in-VES-tuh-gay-shuhnz)* acts of looking into something carefully in order to find facts and get information ***(page 2)***

oceanographer *(oh-shuh-NAH-gruh-fuhr)* a scientist who studies the ocean ***(page 12)***

seabed *(SEE-bed)* the ocean floor ***(page 2)***

sewage *(SEW-ij)* waste that is carried off from sinks, toilets, and other devices ***(page 5)***

software *(SAWFT-wayr)* programs used by a computer to perform tasks ***(page 12)***

submersible *(suhb-MUHR-suh-buhl)* something that can go under water ***(page 11)***

Index

Amundsen, Roald, *7*
bean plant growth experiment, *19–21*
explosives, *9*
fertilizer, *19–21*
helicopters, *9*
McMurdo Station, *5, 6, 15*
penguins, *7*
pollution, *5*
protective clothing, *2, 6*
SCINI, *11–17*
Scott, Robert, *7*
seabed
–ecology, *4*
–life, *2, 4, 5, 16*
–samples, *17*
seasons in Antarctica, *7, 12*
snowmobiles, *14*
South Pole, *6, 7*
Weddell seals, *10*

Focus on Science

Purpose To investigate how much water a plant needs for healthy growth

Procedure

Step 1 Work with a partner. Reread the experiment on pages 19 to 21. In your experiment, give the plants different amounts of water instead of different amounts of fertilizer.

Step 2 Plant four groups of beans in the same way as described in the experiment.

Step 3 Each day, give Group A no water at all, Group B one teaspoon of water, Group C three teaspoons of water, and Group D six teaspoons of water. When the beans begin to grow, measure the height of each plant every day. Record your measurements.

Step 4 After the beans have been growing for two weeks, measure each plant. Decide how much water is best for growing beans.

Conclusion What have you learned about the effect of water on growing beans?